INDIANA

A Turner Educational Services, Inc. book. Based on the Portrait
of America television series created by R.E. (Ted) Turner.

Library of Congress Number: 85-9977

3 4 5 6 7 8 9 10   99 98 97 96 95 94 93 92 91 90

Library of Congress Cataloging in Publication Data

Thompson, Kathleen.
  Indiana.

  (Portrait of America)
  "A Turner book."
  Summary: Discusses the history, economy, culture,
and future of Indiana. Also includes a state
chronology, pertinent statistics, and maps.
  1. Indiana—Juvenile literature. [1. Indiana]
I. Title. II. Series: Thompson, Kathleen. Portrait of
America.
F526.3.T46   1985   977.2   85-9977
ISBN 0-86514-430-3 (lib. bdg.)
ISBN 0-86514-505-9 (softcover)

Cover Photo: Balthazar Korab

★ ★ ★ ★ ★
Portrait of AMERICA

INDIANA

Kathleen Thompson

A TURNER BOOK
RAINTREE PUBLISHERS

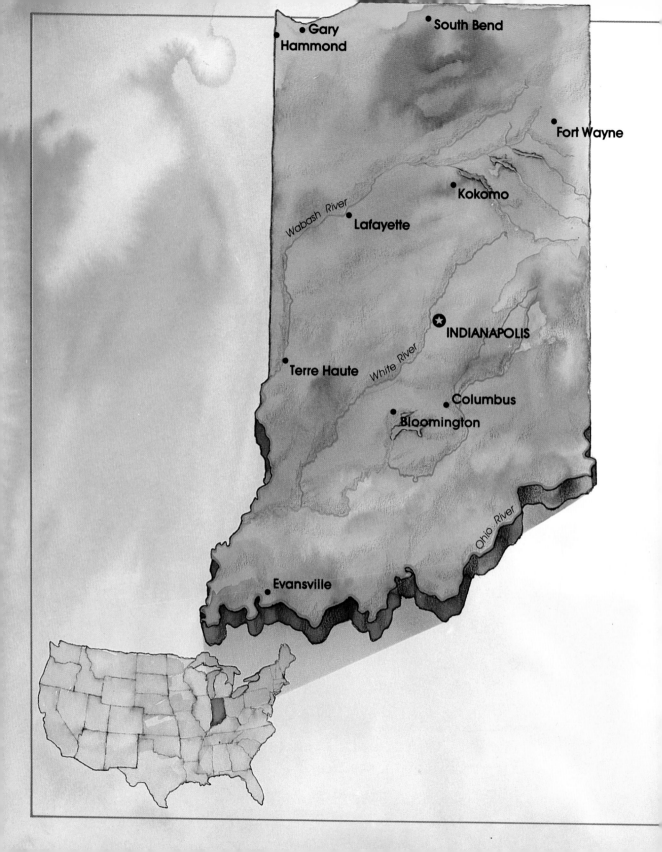

CONTENTS

Introduction

"**I**ndiana is pure America. If you want to know the real, true American character, this is home base."

Indiana, the Main Street of the Midwest.

"I've traveled all over the United States and when I come back to Indiana, I feel that the people here in Indiana have their feet on the ground."

Indiana, the Crossroads of America.

"It's just a way of life. The land keeps you if you keep it."

Indiana shows many different faces to the world. It is a land of cornfields and car races, limestone quarries and literary giants, farms and factories. But perhaps the most important thing about Indiana is that the contradictions, when you look closely, don't seem to be contradictions at all. They seem to fit somehow into a special kind of spirit.

Here, new things are not welcomed simply because they

The Billie Creek Bridge—one of the thirty-five covered bridges in Parke County.

are new. And they are not feared either. They are tested, to see whether they can be used and enjoyed. And if they can, they become part of the Indiana way of life.

Indiana, the Hoosier state, has long had an image of hard work and traditional values, of farms and back roads and families sitting quietly on front porches, rocking or swinging slowly on an old porch swing. And that's part of what Indiana really is. But it's not the whole picture.

The people of Indiana like that image. They cherish it and joke about it. But Indiana is also the steel mills of Gary, the fast cars of the Indianapolis 500, the opera at Indiana University. It is a state where the past lives side by side with the future. And that special Indiana spirit makes it work.

An old church, a violin-playing contest at a holiday celebration, a farm . . . create one image of what Indiana really is.

From Indians
to the Indy

First there were the Mound Builders, Indians of prehistoric times. Then, in Indiana, there were the Miami —and later the Delaware, Mohican, Shawnee, Muncee . . . the Piankashaw, Kickapoo, Wea, and Huron. They hunted and trapped. They lived off the wealth of a land of thick forests and clear lakes.

In 1679, the French explorer La Salle came. He saw the good hunting and trapping. He also saw a short route between the Mississippi and the Great Lakes, important for carrying furs back to the east. Soon trappers and traders were moving through and into Indian land. First there were the French, then the English. Then the wars.

In 1763, the French gave the Indiana region to the British,

These Indians are performing a harvest dance at a
Feast of the Harvest Moon celebration.

but the Indians did not agree. They continued to fight. Eventually, the British reserved all the land west of the Appalachian Mountains to the Indians and guaranteed religious and other freedoms to French settlers.

This time someone else did not agree—the English colonists who had begun to call themselves American. During the American Revolution, a man named George Rogers Clark won important posts in Indiana. When the war ended, the territory belonged to the new United States. There would be more Indiana opposition, but Indiana Territory was formed, with William Henry Harrison as governor.

The Shawnee chief Tecumseh fought valiantly to keep Indian lands, but he was defeated in 1811 in the Battle of Tippecanoe. By 1815, the land had been taken by settlers of European heritage.

In 1816, Indiana became the nineteenth state of the United States of America.

The settlements in Indiana then were few and far apart. Each community depended almost completely on itself to fill

These cabins have been reconstructed to look like those in New Harmony in the early 1800s.

its own needs.

By 1850, there was a state constitution. There were towns, roads, schools, and churches. There were local governments and political parties. And there were some brave experiments in new ways of life.

A group called the Harmony Society, led by George Rapp, started a community called Harmonie. In 1825, it became New

Harmony. The community tried new rules for living together, new ideas for science and education. Even though the experiment failed, New Harmony brought scholars, teachers, and scientists to Indiana.

In 1851, the second state constitution was adopted. That constitution still stands. It showed the mixed feelings of the people of Indiana towards black Americans. Slavery was declared il-legal in one part of the constitution. But another article stated that no more Negroes would be allowed to enter the state. The federal courts ruled that this article was illegal, but it was not removed from the constitution until 1881.

In the Civil War, Indiana supported the Union. Two hundred thousand Indiana soldiers, mostly volunteers, fought in the Union armies.

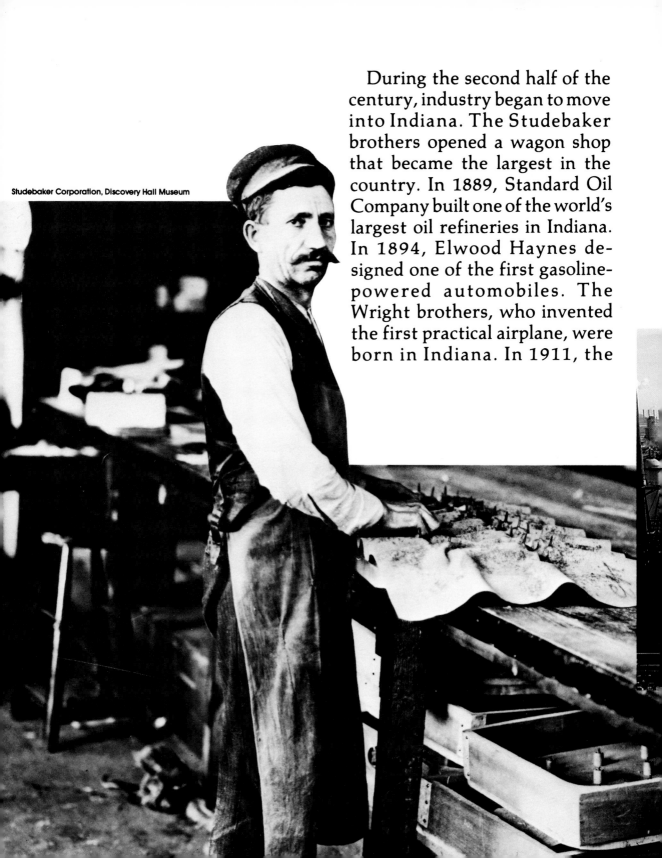

Studebaker Corporation, Discovery Hall Museum

During the second half of the century, industry began to move into Indiana. The Studebaker brothers opened a wagon shop that became the largest in the country. In 1889, Standard Oil Company built one of the world's largest oil refineries in Indiana. In 1894, Elwood Haynes designed one of the first gasoline-powered automobiles. The Wright brothers, who invented the first practical airplane, were born in Indiana. In 1911, the first 500-mile Memorial Day automobile race—the Indy 500—was run in Indianapolis.

More and more, the people of Indiana moved from the farms to the cities. But farming remained strong and with it the values and traditions of the country people. In the north, Indiana was an important industrial state. All over Indiana, farmers made extra money working in the factories. And people who worked in industry built homes in the rural areas to enjoy the beauty and peace of the land.

In 1940, an Indiana Republican named Wendell Wilkie ran against Franklin Roosevelt for president of the United States. Wilkie lost the election, but he had made a strong stand for ideas that many people in Indiana and the rest of the United States believed in.

In 1967, Richard G. Hatcher became the first black mayor of a major American city when he was elected in Gary.

Today, there is great growth in Indiana. But there are also problems. Changes are bringing a need for different ways of doing things. In 1970, Indianapolis and Marion County were reorganized so that most of the county was included in the city boundaries. This move made it possible to deal more efficiently with some of the economic and social problems of the area.

And many more changes are taking place in the land that has seen Tecumseh, LaSalle, and the Indianapolis 500.

Amoco Oil Company

The photograph at the left was taken in about 1905. It shows a harness worker at the Studebaker factory. Above is the Amoco oil refinery at Whiting. When the first Whiting refinery was built, in 1889, it was one of the world's largest.

An Indiana Lifetime

Ansel Toney was born before the twentieth century was, on a farm in Indiana. He's not a typical Hoosier. Actually, there isn't a typical Hoosier, anymore than there's a typical American. But his life shows a lot that Indiana was and is.

Ansel Toney's great-great-great-grandfather came over from England—to farm. His children worked on the farm and so did their children. Ansel Toney was a boy on the farm when the first automobile was manufactured. He was a young man when industry began moving into Indiana in a big way.

But things that were new and different were not frightening. They were exciting. And they were to be used.

Ansel Toney is shown at the far right. The farmer at the near right is sideraking hay. His sideraker is much like ones that were used about the time Ansel Toney was born.

Richard D. Hawthorne

16

At the far right is Ansel Toney's grandson with his wife. At the top is one of Ansel's kites. Above is a modern Indiana farm.

"I bought one of the first combines that was made, and I bought one of the first corn pickers that was made, and I bought one of the first tractors that was made—back in 1913 I bought the first tractor. But think of what we've got now—a tractor that one boy can do more work with than forty men with a hundred and twenty head of horses."

Ansel Toney married, had children and grandchildren, and

worked the land. He saw highways being built for fast new cars. He watched farms change from small family affairs to big businesses. He watched his grandson, Doug, leave the farm for college and a career in journalism. And he watched Doug come back to the land.

Now Doug works on the family farm. He is also the agricultural editor of a nearby newspaper, working to make things better for the farmers of his area.

In his ninety-fifth year, Ansel Toney has a new interest. He makes kites. He finds the same kind of satisfaction in his original designs and his carefully made, brightly colored kites that he found in farming.

"The way I feel about life is that I've always wanted to be creative, wanted to make things, build things . . ."

This love for the old and excitement about the new is part of what makes Indiana, and the people who live there, a special part of America.

"Things have changed so fast. . . . And I don't know what to think of it. It's going to get pretty complicated after awhile. But it's a great time to live."

Corn, Limestone, and Literature

Indiana is the smallest state west of the Appalachian mountains, except for Hawaii. In fact, it's only the thirty-eighth largest state in the United States and it's the smallest state in the Midwest. But . . .

Indiana is the twelfth largest state in the country in population. It's one of the ten leading states in farming *and* manufacturing. And, for some reason, Indiana produces a lot of famous writers.

No one knows for sure about why the writers developed. The other things are a little easier to explain.

First, the farming. The land in Indiana is rich and fertile. The climate is ideal for raising most grain crops. There is plenty of water in the hundreds of natural lakes as well as a

An oxygen-furnace control pit.

Corn is Indiana's biggest crop.

good yearly rainfall. But more important perhaps than all of that, is the fact that the people who came from Europe to settle here had a long agricultural tradition. They knew farming and they loved it. Originally most of the state—seven-eighths of it—was covered with forests. But thousands of acres of trees were destroyed to clear the land for farming. The vast treeless plains that are covered with corn didn't start out that way.

Corn is the biggest crop. At one time, Indiana was called the land of "corn, limestone, and literature." Now, farmers also grow soybeans, wheat, and other crops such as hay, oats, rye,

tobacco, barley, and popcorn.

Farmers in Indiana raise hogs, too, and cattle. Indiana doesn't have Wisconsin's reputation as a dairy producer, but milk is a leading farm product in the state.

Until World War I, Indiana remained primarily a farming state. But industry had already begun to move into the state in the second half of the nineteenth century. After the first world war, manufacturing moved ahead of agriculture. Today, manufactured products make up 84 percent of all the goods produced in Indiana. Farm products make up about 13 percent. In 1920, just over half of Indiana's

U.S. Steel Corporation

Delco Electronics

Indiana's largest industry is steel manufacturing (left). The inset shows a "clean room" at a plant that manufactures thousands of tiny, electronic integrated circuits (ICs) each day.

population lived in its cities. By 1980, almost two-thirds had moved into urban areas.

Indiana produces more steel than corn, now. Gary has some of the country's largest steel mills. Every year, the state produces about 23 million tons of raw steel.

Indiana also turns steel and other raw materials into aircraft engines, transportation equipment, automobile parts. In most General Motors cars, the doors are from Marion, the four-cylinder aluminum-block-engine is from Bedford, and the small computer units under the hood are from Kokomo. Detroit may make the cars, but Indiana makes the parts that make the cars.

The Indy

Long, low cars streak past on the oval track. Spectators, banked high on all sides, cheer in the bright Indiana sunshine. The Indiana Motor Speedway is a blur of high octane and high spirits.

"I have to wear the suit and tie all year long. It's a release—to get out here and get a little crazy: don't hurt anybody and have a good time."

In Indiana people—farmers, factory workers, business executives—have made the Indianapolis 500 a part of their lives and their state.

"Oh, it's a tradition. I've been coming here for fifteen years. It gets in your

blood.''

Since 1911, Indiana and the world have celebrated the power and excitement of the automobile here in Indianapolis. The first Indy 500 was won by a car that averaged seventy-five miles an hour. Now, the strangely streamlined racers hit two hundred miles an hour, and the Indy has become the largest single-day sporting event in the entire world.

For the people of Indiana, this mammoth car race is more than just a good time in the open air. It's a symbol of the place the automobile and its motor-driven relatives have taken in the life of the state.

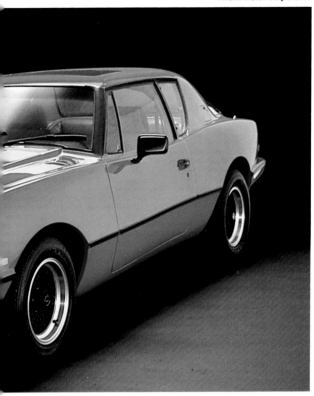

Steve Blake, the chief executive officer of Avanti, is shown with one of the company's cars.

On the farms, tractors changed everything from the tilling of the soil to the harvesting of the crops. Fewer people working fewer hours could produce more and more food to feed, not just the farmer and the community, but the world.

And the Hoosiers enjoy it.

"I love the power—just the feeling you get on the tractor. You let it go, and you give it the throttle, and you are gone—just a total feeling of control."

In the factories and the research laboratories, automobile technology has become an important part of the Indiana economy. Research is going on to make an engine that won't need cooling or lubrication. Computer technology that will help make cars that "think for themselves" is being explored. At the Avanti factory, in South Bend, workers make one of the world's finest cars.

"We are so small that we make as many cars in a year as General Motors makes every four minutes. And, as you can see, they are working ridiculous hours—for a reason. This isn't a job to them. It's a labor of love."

Four wheels, six wheels, or the big eighteen. If it has an engine, the Hoosiers know what to do with it.

Culture:
The Indiana
Surprise Party

About a hundred years ago, there was a livery stable owner in Peru, Indiana, whose name was Benjamin Wallace. Whenever a circus came to town, it would need a lot of things from Wallace's livery stable—and a lot of other stores in town. The circus would pay when it left, if there was enough money. Of course, the store owners didn't just trust these traveling circus people so, until the owners got their money, they removed and kept the nuts that held the wheels on the circus wagons. If the circus made enough money to pay its bills, it got the nuts back and could move on. Making money to pay expenses was called "making the nut." And the phrase is still used today in much of the show business world.

A 1935 poster announcing the Hagenbeck-Wallace circus.

Well, one circus didn't make its nut in Peru, Indiana, and Benjamin Wallace, livery store owner, found himself the proud owner of a circus. That was the beginning of a long history of circuses in Indiana. In 1934, the Hagenback/Wallace circus was one of the biggest in the country.

Clyde Beatty trained his big cats in Peru. Tom Mix spent the winter there. Today, Peru has an amateur circus that performs for two weeks every summer. Its performers are children from the town along with some adults— local business and professional people—who just love the circus.

But circus organs sound only one of the many notes in Indiana's special song. And here again, Indiana is a surprise. One of the things that Hoosiers love most is . . . opera.

In Bloomington, Indiana University is one of the great opera centers of this country. The music school is the biggest in the nation, and it is rated number one. The school's opera company is the first school group ever invited to the Metropolitan Opera in New York.

Thousands of musical per-

An opera production at Indiana University.

formances are given every year in Bloomington by orchestras, bands, small musical groups, and solo performers.

And then there are the writers. Some of the great names of American literature belong to Hoosiers. Theodore Dreiser, author of the novel *An American Tragedy*. Booth Tarkington, author of *The Magnificent Ambersons*. Kurt Vonnegut, author of *Cat's Cradle*.

Cole Porter, the great songwriter, came from Indiana and so did another great writer of American songs, Hoagie Carmichael.

Indiana entertainers include comedians Red Skelton and David Letterman and actress Carole Lombard.

At the left is an assembly line at the Cummins Engine Company. J. Irwin Miller (below, left), the president of Cummins, was reponsible for the many buildings in Columbus that were designed by some of the world's great architects. The North Christian Church (below, right) is one example of Columbus's architecture.

And Indiana is not just a place where fine artists are born. It is a place that encourages art in many ways. Painters, for example, love the rolling hills of Brown County. And, in a town called Columbus, an unusual corporation has created a very special place for art.

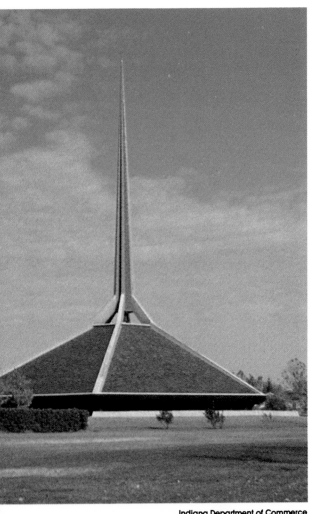

Indiana Department of Commerce

The Beauty of Columbus

Columbus, Indiana, is a town with one major industry. It is the home of Cummins, the country's leading maker of diesel engines. Most of the people in the town make their living, directly or indirectly, because the Cummins factories are there.

But Cummins has brought more to Columbus than factories. All over the city are buildings designed by the great architects of the world.

"Columbus, Indiana, is the only place in the whole world where you can look at an Eero Saarinen church through a Henry Moore arch in front of an I.M. Pei library."

The man behind this unusual contribution to the beauty of an Indiana town is J. Irwin Miller of the Cummins Engine Company. It is an expression of his religion.

"It has always been clear to me that the Christian message, or the Christian gospel, is transmitted in many ways and that words alone are not adequate. It's transmitted through architecture; it's transmitted through music, through poetry, drama, and in all the ways that mankind has discovered to express feelings."

Of course, the extraordinary buildings of Columbus are not just for looking at. They are places where the people live their lives. They are churches and schools and libraries. They create an unusual environment for the work and play of the citizens of the town.

"When I look at our schools now, since all the new architecture has come along, and I move into those buildings and work with the teachers and kids, I know absolutely that these buildings have got to make a difference in their lives . . . and not only in that day's work, but I think they carry that out of the building, too."

Columbus, and the Cummins contribution to its architecture, are another example of the spirit of Indiana. While they treasure the past, they live comfortably with the future.

On the right-hand page are two of Columbus's elementary schools. Columbus educators feel that the architecture of the buildings helps the students' schoolwork.

A Move Toward a Better Life

"Well, it all started in the fourth grade. Well, Mr. Cotter, he asked us did we want to play chess. And we said, 'Why should we play chess?'"

For a group of Indianapolis children, that question has been answered in an inspiring way. Robert Cotter, a classroom teacher, brought together a group of inner-city kids and a chessboard with spectacular results.

"We entered a tournament in November. We finished dead last, losing nineteen out of twenty games, and that's when people came to me and said, 'Hey, there is no way you can ever do anything with these kids. This game is too difficult. It's too complicated.' And that inspired me and I was able to convey that message to the kids, and it also inspired them."

Robert Cotter did his job well enough so that his group of eleven- and twelve-year-olds won the national public school chess championship. From there they went to Washington, D.C., to the White House.

"I think the best thing that's happened is going to Washington, D.C., to meet the president. Not many people meet the president, and not many even get to see the White House. And it was just—I liked that the best."

When they came back to Indianapolis, the kids were honored by their fellow citizens. Kiwanis Club members welcomed them to a meeting, talked to them, and expressed pride in the students' achievement.

"The expectation is all-important. The expectation: What do we expect out of the children, whether it's in elementary school or junior high school or high school? By and large, that expectation will be realized."

It took independent thinking to put chess pieces into the hands of children who had never seen them before. It took determination for those children to overcome their first failures with the game and go on to master it. But those are two things that the people of Indiana have never been short on.

Robert Cotter playing chess with some of his students.

Looking Forward

The people of Indiana have ideas for their future. They have dreams that, considering what they have accomplished so far, seem very likely to come true.

Mayor Richard Hatcher is trying to make Gary a center of black history and culture.

"One of the alternatives we are looking at is the idea of turning Gary into a major convention center. Now, normally, people would laugh at that . . . 'Gary, Indiana—smokestacks—that's impossible.' What most people don't realize about Gary is that it has so many very wonderful tourist attractions. . . . It may be the best-kept secret in the country."

And it is true. There, between the giant mills, are the beautiful beaches and shifting sands.

The Indiana Sand Dunes.

In Indianapolis, they have just completed the Hoosier Dome. And they've begun to build White River State Park. It will be a huge theme park, like Disneyland. But it will be the first theme park dedicated to physical fitness and health.

White River is part of Indiana's great love for sports and athletics, especially amateur athletics. This is a state where 18,000 people will turn out for a high school basketball game three months after the season is over.

Mayor Richard Hatcher of Gary, a view of Indiana industry, and the Hoosier Dome.

"It's a rah-rah thing in high school and college. You're playing for the fun of it, but you still want to win. You are playing for your school, you're playing for your family, you're playing for your town. . . ."

The state of Indiana is determined to make Indianapolis the amateur sports capital of the world.

Computer technology is part of the future in Indiana's automobile industry, too.

"I think we've suffered sort of a second Pearl Harbor, and the Japanese have once more awakened the sleeping giant . . . for the automotive industry, and we've reached the point where we can put ten thousand transistors on a piece of silicon equal to the diameter of the head of a pin."

The tradition of craftsmanship and skill that began in the days of wood and stone has continued in the era of silicon.

There is another way of looking toward the future, too. It's as much a part of Indiana as the Hoosier Dome or the computer. It's a future that comes in a direct line out of the past.

"I look forward to the time when maybe I can be like Grandpa. Maybe I can sit back and look at a grandchild or a child, and I'll be able to see part of him. I'll be able to tell them how strong Grandpa was, as he told me about his grandfather. It's an amazing thing to think about. And it will probably drive home when I see a baby put in the crib that marks the fourth generation in the same bed. Maybe that's what I'll know. That's the fun of looking ahead."

Ansel Toney's grandson and great granddaughter.

Important Historical Events in Indiana

1679 The French explorer LaSalle crosses Indiana on the St. Joseph and Kankakee rivers.

1704-1732 The French build three trading posts: Fort Miami, Fort Ouiatenon, and Vincennes.

1763 The French and Indian War ends with a treaty. Indiana is ceded to Great Britain by France.

1779 George Rogers Clark establishes control of Vincennes.

1783 Indiana is included in the area ceded to the United States after the American Revolution.

1787 Indiana becomes part of the Northwest Territory.

1800 The Indiana Territory is established with Vincennes as the capital. William Henry Harrison is the first territorial governor.

1811 William Henry Harrison defeats Indians at the Battle of Tippecanoe near Lafayette.

1813 The territorial capital is moved to Corydon.

1815 George Rapp, leader of the Harmony Society, establishes a communal settlement called Harmonie.

1816 Indiana becomes the nineteenth state on December 11.

1825 Robert Owen takes over Harmonie and renames it New Harmony.

1894 Elwood Haynes builds an early automobile in Kokomo.

1906 The city of Gary is founded by the United States Steel Corporation.

1911 The first Memorial Day 500-mile automobile race is held at Indianapolis.

1933 The state government is reorganized; the governor receives greater powers.

1956 The Northern Indiana Toll Road is completed.

1963 The Studebaker Corporation ends automobile production.

1965 The Indiana Department of Natural Resources is created to handle problems of soil erosion and water pollution.

1966 The Indiana Sand Dunes National Lakeshore is established.

1967 Richard D. Hatcher is elected mayor of Gary, becoming Indiana's first black mayor.

Indiana Almanac

Nickname. The Hoosier State.

Capital. Indianapolis.

State Bird. Cardinal.

State Flower. Peony.

State Tree. Tulip Tree.

State Motto. The Crossroads of America.

State Song. On the Banks of the Wabash.

State Abbreviations. Ind. (traditional); IN (postal).

Statehood. December 11, 1816, the 19th state.

Government. Congress: U.S. senators, 2; U.S. representatives, 10. **State Legislature:** senators, 50; representatives, 100. **Counties:** 92.

Area. 36,291 sq. mi. (93,993 sq. km.), 38th among the states.

Greatest Distances. north/south, 280 mi. (451 km.); east/west, 160 mi. (257 km.). **Shoreline:** 45 mi. (72 km.), on Lake Michigan.

Elevation. Highest: Wayne Couny, 1,257 ft. (383 m). **Lowest:** Ohio River, 320 ft. (98 m).

Population. 1980 Census: 5,490,224 (5.7% increase over 1970), twelfth among the states. **Density:** 151 persons per sq. mi. (58 persons per sq. km.). **Distribution:** 64% urban, 36% rural. **1970 Census:** 5,195,392.

Economy. Agriculture: hogs, cattle, corn, soybeans. **Manufacturing:** primary metals, transporation equipment, electrical machinery. **Mining:** coal, stone, petroleum.

Places to Visit

Brown County Art Galleries.
Conner Prairie Pioneer Settlement.
George Rogers Clark Memorial.
Indiana Dunes State Park.
Lincoln Pioneer Village.
New Harmony.
Parke County.

Annual Events

Maple Fair in Rockville (February).
Indiana High School basketball tournament (March).
Indianapolis 500-mile Memorial Day Automobile Race.
Bluegrass Music Festival in Beanblossom (June).
Circus Day Festival in Peru (July).
Indiana State Fair in Indianapolis (August).
Parke County Covered Bridge Festival in Rockville (October).

Indiana Counties

© American Map Corporation
License 18920

47

INDEX

977.2   Thompson, Kathleen
THOMPSON   Indiana

	DATE DUE		
FEB 28			
FEB 8			
D-5			
MAR 22			
MAY 10